⊶⟶ The Beautiful ⟵⊷
People of Kenya

Mohamed Amin·Duncan Willetts·Brian Tetley

Camerapix Publishers Limited

This edition published 1997 by
Camerapix Publishers Limited
PO Box 45048
Nairobi
Kenya

First published 1989

Second impression 1997

© Camerapix 1989

ISBN 1 874041 92 X

This book was designed and produced by
Camerapix Publishers Limited
PO Box 45048, Nairobi, Kenya

Design: Craig Dodd
Typeset: Nazma Rawji

Printed in Hong Kong by South China Printing Co. (1988) Ltd.

Contents

Introduction

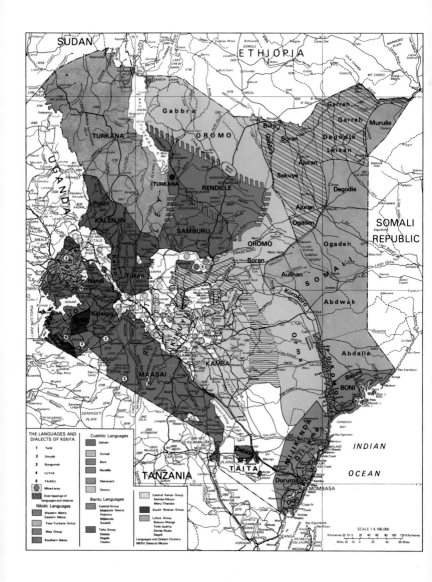

THE LANGUAGES AND DIALECTS OF KENYA

1 Terik
2 Omotik
3 Bongomek
4 LUYIA
5 YAAKU
○ Mixed area
⟨⟨⟩⟩ Over lappings of
languages and dialects

Nilotic Languages
- Western Nilotic
- Eastern Nilotic
- Teso-Turkana Group
- Maa Group
- Southern Nilotic

Cushitic Languages
- Dahalo
- Somali
- Boni
- Rendille
- Daasanach
- Oromo

Bantu Languages
- Coastal Group
  Mijikenda
  Miji Swana
  Pokomo
  Swahili
- Taita Group
  Dabida
  Segala
  Taveta
- Central Kenya Group
  Kamba-Kikuyu
  Meru-Tharaka
- South Nyanza Group
- Luhya Group
  Bukusu-Wanga
  Tiriki-Isukha
  Samia-Nyala
  Ragoli
  Languages and Dialect Clusters
  MERU Dialects Mutini

SCALE 1:4,166,000

Kilometres 20 10 0   20   40   60   80   100   120 Kilometres
Miles 20 10 0   20   40   60 Miles

Introduction

For centuries, people from many parts of Africa have been migrating to Kenya's broad, pleasant, and sunny half-a-million square kilometres of snow-capped mountain, fertile plain, bushy savannah, desert, and palm-fringed coral coast. Each has brought some distinctive feature of their own culture and language to add to Kenya's colourful mosaic of mankind. This melting-pot of peoples, a vibrant community of twenty-two million citizens, will reach almost forty million by the turn of the century.

Spread all across this vast land astride the Equator, many have had to adapt their cultures and customs to the terrain in which they live – sometimes green and fertile, often harsh and arid. Indeed, ironically, the smallest group, the Cushitic-speaking Kenyans, occupy the largest area. The nomads of the north, who roam almost half the country, make up only three per cent of the population.

For most, two-thirds of all Kenyans, the common tongue is that of the Bantu languages. The remainder speak Nilotic languages. But these three language structures bind a country of more than forty different ethnic groups – 'tribes' if you like, though that word only defines a group because they live in one place and have a distinct culture – which make up the *Beautiful People of Kenya*.

All those who have migrated here during the last 4,000 years have assimilated something of those who were already here, including the earliest ancestors of modern man who took their first faltering footsteps on the shores of Lake Turkana, a vast inland water in Kenya's north known as the 'Jade Sea'.

If historical perspective has any accuracy, Turkana's bleak eastern shore is the one place on earth which can rightly be regarded as Eden, that lush cornucopia of Biblical legend which,

7

in reality, is now a land of knife-edge lava wastes and petrified forests.

From Ileret in the north to beyond Alia Bay in the south, and for several miles inland, Koobi Fora's antediluvian fossil beds have provided the most significant clues yet to mankind's beginnings. They have earned Koobi Fora the name *Cradle of Mankind*.

Nowadays the lush imagery of Eden is nowhere in evidence and the paucity of food and potential profit is counterpoint to the wealth of humankind which still exists in this region – living societies which serve as rich and colourful reminders of what mankind arose from and of his initial struggle for survival.

The land yields little. The soil is worn out or eroded by wind and water. The people are hardy, spartan and indifferent to the materialism which has assailed the rest of the world.

The only profit for which they care is survival. Staying alive is indicative of a wealth of human resourcefulness – and a reflection of the initiative and fellowship which characterize all the *Beautiful People of Kenya*.

With a 1989 population of twenty-two million, Kenya is also one of the youngest nations in the world: the majority are under thirty years of age with all that this implies in terms of human resources and initiative.

They form a cultural tapestry without compare in the twentieth-century – a group of varied and different origins homogenised as one people, one nation.

Adopting the benefits of modern technology and education, and adapting them to fit their own ageless structures of justice and democracy, Kenya's peoples go endlessly about their many lawful enterprises in a colourful pageant of free-wheeling businesses and mercantile initiatives allied to long hours of industriousness and labour all over this sunny, carefree nation.

Minority migrant groups – the Arabs, Asians, and Europeans – have all been absorbed into the mainstream of society to make their own contribution to the national well-being.

And though many of the traditions of the past are now ended, or in the process of replacement, this book is intended to serve as an insight into the proud and glorious histories of the more than forty individual societies that combine to make up one single identity – the beautiful people of this unique land.

We wish to thank Alastair Matheson, Daniel Stiles, and Dr Taaitta Toweett, for reading this manuscript and making many useful suggestions.

Half–title: Rendille woman with coxcomb denoting birth of her first son. Title page: Maasai manyatta in Amboseli. Contents page: Gabbra nomad with camels loaded with mobile home crosses the north–eastern deserts of Kenya.

Below: Traditional Taita music group.

One · People of Plain and Mountain

In the span of eighty years, a single lifetime, the people of Kenya have had to absorb the impact of cultural and technological innovations which took other societies thousands of years to assimilate. They succeeded beyond belief. Sons of peasant farmers have become masters of the skies at the controls of wide-body jets. The offspring of pastoral nomads are doctors of philosophy in the arts of computer science. The sorcerer's grandson edits an influential daily newspaper typeset by photographic images and printed, web offset, at the rate of 80,000 copies an hour.

Yet it was barely more than a century ago – in 1883 – that the first of the European travellers penetrated the hinterland of East Africa, until then the most isolated of any of the world's major regions. Just ninety years ago the first line of the 1,000–kilometre-long Mombasa to Lake Victoria railway track was laid. The sudden advent of so much in so brief a time – Kenya became a free independent nation at the beginning of the Space Age – has had not only profoundly disturbing implications for Kenyan society but also blessings.

If, inevitably, it has brought the avarice of other societies based on the materialism of industries and cash economies and the reprise of weapons that can kill at the touch of a finger, it has also come with such swiftness it has had no time to erode the time-honoured traditions and established patterns of life.

To the delight of all, good, ageless proven ways, cultures, and customs still prevail in Kenya, though sometimes to the despair of those who regard the refusal of the Maasai to wear tie, shirt, and suit as not so much an affirmation of ethnic warriorhood but more an expression of primitive and chauvinistic ignorance.

Yet, striding across the dusty plains, clad only in loose-flowing red robe, spear in hand, skin oiled and gleaming, hair slicked down with a spat of 'Brylcreem' ochre, the **Maasai** initiate is the very celebration of the romantic cliche of the African warrior: the epitome of grace and nobility, an ancient aristocrat often thought to be one of the lost legions of Anthony.

Certainly no other community in Kenya has had so much written or observed about them as these nomadic pastoralists, who swept south to their present home during the last 500 years.

Today, set flush alongside the Kenya-Tanzania border from Ntimaru in the west to Oloitokitok in the east, Kenya's 250,000 Maasai pastoralists no longer roam free as they used to. Their range in the north-east ends around the Chyulu Hills and in the north-west stops on the forbidding brow of the Mau Escarpment.

A thousand years or more ago, their Nilotic forebears were intermarrying with people of Cushitic stock in the area north-west of Turkana. Moving steadily south, raiding and pillaging as they went, they acquired large herds, a fearsome reputation, and dominated a vast territory. They reached their apogee in the middle of the nineteenth century – feared and respected by all who came across them, including the first European visitors.

It was not only the noble mien of the warriors and the comely appearance of the young Maasai maidens which earned the admiration of strangers, but also their seemingly loose yet closely-knit social structures. Made up of five (some say it is seven) clans, each divided into units marked by the emblem of their cattle brand, Maasai society is an inflexible autocracy. Each level is decided by the promotion of successive generations to new positions of responsibility.

The chief autocrat of the entire community is the *laibon* – a

11

Above: Initiates with ostrich feather headdresses denoting warrior status perform triumphal dance as youngsters join in.

Opposite: Vividly coloured traditional Maasai necklaces and head jewellery.

Right: Maasai warrior – morani.

seer, soothsayer, or visionary – who decides when the time is right for the tribe's intricate and elaborate age-group rituals by which each generation is elevated to a new level of seniority. Ultimately, the oldest relinquish all power and retire to become venerable and highly respected wise men.

Each level is characterized by a name. For instance, the two fighting cadres – the youngest and fittest of the generations and the most elite – junior and senior warriors, are known as *il-moran*. They are bound to each other by a lifelong oath administered during the initiation ceremonies when they are ushered into manhood. This passage from childhood to junior warrior is marked by circumcision.

Most sacred of all the Maasai social rituals, the ceremony takes place every twelve to fifteen years, according to the movement of the stars and planets in the southern skies. The initiate is prepared for the ceremony by his mother, who shaves his head. He is bathed with milk as a blessing for the ordeal he is about to face.

His bond partners hold his legs apart as the circumciser goes about his business. No matter how intense the pain, the initiate must never flinch. Not so much by the tremor of an eyelid must he indicate discomfort, for to do so would bring disgrace upon himself, his family, and his clan.

The cut takes a minute, the initiation lasts a month. During this time the new initiates roam the bush in black robes shooting down birds with blunt arrowheads tipped with resin gum. These are fashioned into diadem head-dresses, striking proof of hunting prowess and symbol of newfound manhood.

These years of conscription, now only symbolically in the tribe's service, are carefree. Although forbidden during their warrior period to marry, the young warriors lead no cloistered life of monastic celibacy. The youngest and prettiest of the uncircumcised maidens, known as *entito*, are theirs to enjoy – but not to make pregnant.

But Maasai life, a series of elaborately orchestrated events, rituals full of fire and colour, is sadly coming to the end of its traditions.

The second stage of a man's life, for instance, is his elevation from warrior to junior elder during a four- to five-day-long pageant inside a specially built enclosure. This almost pure theatre, with its set pieces, closes when the enclosure is ceremonially set on fire and razed to the ground.

During the set pieces within the enclosure, however, the age-mates choose themselves a new leader – a man of flawless physique and outstanding moral character. Their choice is confirmed by the chief laibon, and then the leader, *olutono*, is invited to choose a wife. The bachelor years have ended and the rest follow him in choosing a bride.

In 1988 one of the Maasai clans around Kajiado staged the last of their *eunoto* ceremonies, bringing to an end more than 2,000 years of tradition. The clan's elders, persuaded by the government that the warrior system was retarding development, vowed there would be no more. Not without some sadness, of course.

The Maasai cherish their culture. Even so, more and more of these monarchs of the bush are being encouraged to abandon their nomadic pastoralism and settle down on a farm or smallholding to rear not only cattle but crops. To the traditional, chauvinist Maasai, of course, the idea of crop farming is as abhorrent as the suggestion that he should restrict the size of his herds.

Below: Junior Maasai warriors awaiting the eunoto *ceremony – the moment when they are elevated to senior warriors.*

Opposite: Each bite of roasted meat seals lifelong bond of fidelity between the il–murrani.

Opposite bottom: Smoky interior of a Maasai manyatta.

Long before the Europeans introduced a cash economy, most societies in Africa, and in Kenya in particular, judged a man's wealth either by the number of cattle he owned or the area of land he farmed and the wives he maintained. Life was everything; death, the end of everything.

Even today many Maasai show antipathy to the custom of burying their dead. Traditionally, only the great *laibons* merit a grave. The rest are simply left out in the open bush for the scavengers.

Almost the first introduction any of the early missionaries or travellers had to Kenya's inland tribes were the highly superstitious folk who farmed the verdant, terraced slopes of the 1,821–metre-high Taita Hills and the Maktau Plains at their feet.

These good country folk, the **Taita-Taveta**, revered sacred spirits – none more so than those of their family ancestors whose spirits reposed in the custody of their skulls. Stacked together in a natural shrine, usually a cave, these skulls were a potent force for good or evil.

They were normally taken from the body a few days after burial and wrapped in the leaves of a local plant and then placed in the clan cave. The spirits reposing within the skulls granted special favours to supplicants who prayed before them with earthly sacrifices.

Ranging from the shores of the marsh lake Jipe, along the Tanzanian border, to the crater lake of Chala, high on the slopes of Mount Kilimanjaro, and inland across the Maktau Plains where Tsavo National Park now stands, this community of 200,000 people includes many smaller groups such as the Kasigau, Sagala, and Dabida. Roughly, the Taveta inhabit the plains and the Taita the hills.

18

Divided into seven clans, strict taboos still exist against marriages between members of the same clan. Farming has always been the main occupation – although Taita-Taveta smithies and handicraft workers also established a widespread reputation for their skills. At times almost a religious affair, governed by a sacred ordinance, as well as requiring the blessing of the ruling elders, no land could be turned, nor crops planted, without submission to the spirits.

Inevitably, this involved sacrifices. Not to do so invoked a harvest of despair – dust and famine – for the farmer.

Tribal spirits were, and presumably still are, territorial. Each occupied a well-defined area – guarding those inside the locality from evil influences outside. These spirits were demanding. They wanted not only sacrifices as an augur of a good harvest but as continual appeasement to ward off drought, famine, and personal troubles.

Today, without any sacrifices at all, the Taita-Taveta farmlands burgeon with rich, lush produce; vegetables for the home table and, for the market, cash crops like coffee, tea, bananas, and mangoes.

Traditionally, families live in either a round or square hut made of wooden poles and mud walls with a roof of rafters covered with banana palm thatch. Bachelors have their own home, close to the cattle compound.

Apart from farming, the Taita-Taveta are renowned for their craftsmanship with wood and leather. They are also experts in the making of bows and arrows and preparing the particularly potent local poison to apply to their tips. In the past, these came into swift action when traditional horns sounded, warning of an enemy raid.

Below: Wearing an elegant tiara of cowrie shells and metal chains, a pensive Okiek girl wears a circumcision dress. Initiation is followed by marriage.

Today, active in ranching, farming, and administration, these sturdy, handsome people are in the mainstream of modern Kenyan society, cherishing their ageless traditions but embracing all that is worthwhile of the twentieth century to develop a modern progressive nation.

Would that the same could be said for the colourful remnants of an ancient community now numbering fewer than 10,000 and found only in remote and isolated pockets. Widespread throughout Kenya, diversified by location and distance, now even few Kenyans know much of the **Okiek**, hunters and gatherers of Kenya's highland forests.

Divided into dozens of small, self-contained groups, active in the Mau, Cherangani, Aberdares, and Elgon mountain massifs of the north, for thousands of years these specialists have displayed an uncanny affinity with their environment. Highly mobile, their skills as hunters and trackers – living as one with the flora and fauna on which they depend – have ensured their survival.

They hunted with bows and arrows tipped with a lethal poison prepared by boiling the twigs and leaves of a forest tree (*Akoncanthera*) into a potent stew. Elephant were lured along the floor of the trail until they fell into a deep pit, its bottom lined with bamboo spikes. Occasionally, they moved down off the mountains on to the plains in search of larger antelope. This was when their packs of hunting dogs came into their own, driving the wild beasts towards the traps.

Known to the Maasai and Kikuyu as Wandorobo, the Okiek augment their diet with wild honey, fruit, and vegetables. The women make distinctive pottery, using a technique known as roulette.

Seldom does an Okiek family stay in one place for long. Living in crude, temporary shelters – little more than a bunch of withies placed in the ground and curved to take a covering of skins or bush – they move on every six months or so, trading handicrafts, skins, and honey beer, as they go, for sheep and goats.

In recent years, however, they have begun joining settlements established by other ethnic groups. Many, allocated land and provided with health and social services by a concerned Government, have opted for permanent settlement on their own smallholdings.

Another minority group is the diminutive community known as Njemps, the **Ilchamus** of Lake Baringo. Numbering fewer than 10,000, these people by loss of stock and disease after a severe drought, were forced to leave their Maasai-Samburu kin early in the nineteenth century, and settle down to a steady life of fishing and farming.

Much of their social structure, however, is still based on that of the Maasai – although they have adopted the permanent, round mud-and-wattle huts favoured by their neighbours, the Tuken.

Their circumcision ceremonies are virtually identical to those of the Maasai, but young warriors also have their two lower incisors removed and their stomach scarified. In addition to the traditional Maasai arsenal, they also adopt the lethal wrist and finger knives of the Pokot.

And, although still true to their cattle-keeping traditions – they graze their herds along the lake shore – the Ilchamus have also become resourceful fishermen, casting their nets from the frail, coracle-like rafts which they make from the stems of the ambatch tree and bind together with sansevieria fibre.

Above: Ilchamus children prepare their nets on the rocky shores of Lake Baringo.

Opposite: Ilchamus (Njemps) fisherman, in coracle—like raft made from the stems of the ambatch tree bound together by sansevieria fibre, with the day's catch on Lake Baringo.

Right: Turbanned Ilchamus fishermen in reed bed of crocodile—infested Lake Baringo.

They propel these unlikely craft with two spoon-shaped paddles. As well as fishing, they ferry cattle and passengers across the lake, which is nowhere more than four metres deep. The only real dangers are sudden squalls and the resident colony of Nile crocodile, long believed to be benign to man until one gobbled up an unfortunate fisherman in the 1970s.

Despite its suggestive courtship dance, the community nonetheless has a strong streak of puritanism. Should an uncircumcised girl become pregnant – a grave dishonour to family and clan – the operation is carried out swiftly and, as punishment, ants are placed on the wound.

Normally, a girl is circumcised just before her marriage, which is also the time the families sit down to haggle over the bride price. Days later, dressed in black robe, wearing sandals made by her uncles, her skin greased with goat fat, the girl is escorted to her husband's homestead by her in-laws through two lines of well-wishers who, as a form of blessing, spit on her!

The largest community in Kenya is the **Kikuyu**, whose 3.5 million people have spread all across the country – in business, agriculture, and industry. This thrifty group has made its influence felt from the very top of society to the very bottom.

Made up of nine clans, the traditional homelands of the Kikuyu stretch all the way from the suburbs of Nairobi through Kiambu, Murang'a, Kirinyaga, Karatina, and Nyeri to the foothills of the sacred abode of *Ngai* (God), Mount Kenya, known to the Kikuyu as Kirinyaga.

The tribe began, says the creation legend, in a sacred grove of fig trees near Murang'a where the founder of the tribe, Gikuyu, was sent by Ngai and met Mumbi, the beautiful mother of all the Kikuyu. Their nine daughters are the mothers of the tribe's nine clans.

Although to the casual observer every Kikuyu man seems a self-contained, often swaggering, chauvinistic male, the tribe's culture is based entirely on matriarchal traditions. For instance, when a woman marries, the fire she lights in the traditional three-stone hearth must never be allowed to go out. It would bring misfortune.

The key to Kikuyu philosophy is land: what cattle is to the Maasai and the Samburu, land is to the Kikuyu – the only measure of wealth, prosperity, stability, and happiness.

It was the European regime which alienated some traditional Kikuyu lands and it was this grievance above all which gave rise to the Mau Mau rebellion – mainly disaffected Kikuyu who took to the forest to become guerrillas – and led to Kenya's Independence in 1963.

This was ushered in under the leadership of one of the most traditional yet progressive Kikuyu elders – Mzee Jomo Kenyatta – whose 1938 book *Facing Mount Kenya* was a firm justification of female circumcision and polygamy, both cardinal tenets of Kikuyu society.

Circumcision was necessary if a youth was to join the ranks of warriors and become one of the elders, a generation of various age-sets joined under one name, either Maina or Mwangi, which would hold sway for a period as long as thirty years.

Deeply superstitious about the past, Kikuyu society has embraced every innovation of western trade, industry, and technology and often improved upon it. In the old days this superstition was used to bring the recalcitrant to heel. The most common of these methods was employed by the council of elders, *kiama*, which was the judicial authority of the tribe. When in doubt about an accused person, the elders would

Opposite: Largest of Kenya's ethnic groups, a group of Kikuyu traditional dancers.
Opposite bottom: Agriculturalists by tradition, a Kikuyu mother carries her baby during the coffee-picking season.

Below: Kikuyu matriarch wearing traditional headdress, earrings, and necklaces.

invoke one of two ordeals to determine a person's innocence or guilt. One involved the use of a red-hot knife which was placed in the mouth of the accused. According to the extent of the blistering which the tongue underwent, so was the person adjudged innocent or guilty.

Another system involved a ritual oath-taking over a demonaic seven-holed stone believed to cast potent powers of punishment. This stone was called the *githathi*.

Today Kikuyu elders are more likely to administer the law with the prefix of 'Mr Justice' before their name as one of the judges in the High Court of Kenya, using precedents and procedures laid down long ago by the ancient Romans.

One of the most closely-related ethnic groups to the Kikuyu is the one-million-strong **Meru** community which farms the eastern slopes of Mount Kenya. Made up of eight clans – Chuka, Muthambi, Mwimbi, Igoji, Miutini, Imenti, Tigania, and Igembe – the Meru are an extremely resourceful, innovative, and adept community which has made a niche for itself in every aspect of Kenyan society.

Until fairly recently in historical terms – late in the nineteenth century, in fact – these clans kept very much to themselves, often feuding, fussing, and a'fighting with one another. As a homogenous whole, the Meru community is a relatively new phenomenon.

Socially, their structures are virtually identical to those of the Kikuyu, with one significant difference. Girls who have just been circumcised go into seclusion for certain periods – the longest being that of the Tigania clan, whose female initiates vanish from public view for two years. In the company of an older woman, each initiate is instructed in the arts and duties of a married woman.

During this seclusion, in a special hut, any initiate wishing to move outside must first cover herself completely in a cloak of animal skin. Invariably, the initiate is married the minute the seclusion ends.

Meru villages used to be made up of entire families – three or four generations living as a self-contained unit. Married sons traditionally tacked their own homes on to their father's holdings, as indeed was the case in Kikuyu society. Each wife had her own hut and her own garden, but the bachelors would live in a communal 'mess' where they entertained the young girls.

Blessed with abundant and dependable rainfall, rich and fertile soil, the Meru have turned the lower slopes of the mountain into a veritable granary of wheat and cash crops, vegetables and fruit, herding their cattle on the lower ground. Their mountainside scenery includes waterfalls, caves, forests and a number of lakes, including the sacred lake, Nkunga.

Today these industrious people are leaders of industry, commerce, education, and agriculture, helping to maintain Kenya's position at the forefront of emergent nations.

Down on the plains below Meru, where the River Tana swirls as it broadens out on its long journey to the Indian Ocean, always near to their beloved sacred trees, rocks, and waterfalls, live the 12,000 or so souls who make up the **Tharaka** community, closely related to the Meru.

Fond of dancing, they fashion both drums and beehives out of logs, marking each with the emblem of a particular clan. Tharaka society is composed of five major clans. In addition to their reputation as drummers and beekeepers, they are as much

Below: Chuka drummer of the Meru ethnic group with traditional drum hollowed out of a tree trunk.

Opposite: Hanging granary of a Meru family keeps harvested maize safe from rodents as it dries out in the sun, protected from rain by the sheaths that cover the cobs.

feared as famed for their mastery of witchcraft. The sick and desperate trek long miles, often from the neighbouring land of the Kamba across the Tana, in search of a powerful incantation or potion to cure an illness, remove a curse, or strike down an enemy with a malady.

Little touched by the changing tides of progress and affluence, ill-served by roads, the Tharaka live towards the end of the twentieth century much as they always have done – their schools ill-attended, communications and roads neglected, earning a few shillings from the sale of plaited shopping baskets and goats.

In the main, the witch doctor remains the elite of society – always welcome with his medicine bag of roots, barks, and leaves, and totems of snail and sea shells, together with magic ornaments, calabashes, cow horns, and the inevitable fly whisk. Sacrifices are mandatory and, given the faith, cures guaranteed.

Neighbours of the Meru on the slopes of Mount Kenya and closely related both to them and the Kikuyu are the 250,000 people who form the **Embu** community.

Traditionally a community of hunters and gatherers divided into twenty-six clans, the Embu are now settled farmers, practising mainly their age-old skills as beekeepers, tilling the rich soil on the south-east slopes of the mountain watered by the many fast-flowing streams which merge lower downstream to form the Tana.

Their social structures and circumcision rites, both male and female, are much the same as those of the Kikuyu and the Meru, and even the traditional homestead – with the patriarch's conical, rounded mud-and-thatch *thingira*, a 'men-only' hut – is identical, each wife occupying her own hut around the edge of

34

the enclosure into which the livestock are herded at night for safekeeping.

Once notable elephant hunters – they used to trap them in pits – and skilled craftsmen famed for the art of their blacksmiths, the Embu now pursue careers in many different sections of Kenya society and have transformed their subsistence farming into a highly-developed and profitable agricultural industry, gathering bountiful harvests of many crops including cotton, coffee, tea, pyrethrum, and rice.

Below the heights of Embu lie the sere and withered brushlands bounded on either side by the Tana and Thika Rivers. Progress in this area of 1,600 square kilometres of stunted, semi-arid land is slow. For the 75,000 people of the **Mbeere** group, sharing cultural and historic affiliations with the Embu, have watched time go by, clinging to their traditional ways, reluctant to adopt the tempo of the twentieth century.

Living in close affinity with a broad range of wildlife – even a few elephant and a rare rhino roam here among the buffalo and other plains game – the Mbeere still practise hunting, often using virulent poisons bought from the Kamba and smeared on the tips of their arrows. These are exceptionally well made: Mbeere blacksmiths produce some of Kenya's finest iron work.

Much of their farming still follows traditional practice. Living in small, isolated, and often remote settlements, they use 'digging sticks' to turn the fields for crops of millet and cow-peas. Recently, however, younger farmers have introduced new hybrid maize available from Government centres and experimented with Mexico beans, sugar cane, and bananas. Livestock is on the increase, too.

In this region, famine is familiar. To alleviate its effects, the

35

Above: Embu mother and children at a local market.

Opposite: Young Tharaka girl collecting the day's water from the river.

Right: Embu mother grinding maize into flour.

Mbeere used to barter regularly with their neighbours – the Kikuyu, Kamba, and Embu – exchanging goats, honey, and ironwork for grain and vegetables. Today the barter system has virtually ceased, but the resulting markets that sprang up still flourish.

The most profound effect on traditional Mbeere life, however, has come since the late 1960s with the exploitation of the Tana River through a series of hydroelectric schemes. With the latest of these, Kiambere, has also arrived a good network of roads. Thus, with a population of which more than half are still under twenty, Mbeere society is dramatically poised to step forward in one stride from the nineteenth to the twenty-first century.

This would bring them out of the shadow of their large, powerful, and enterprising neighbours – the two million or more people of the **Kamba** community, one of Kenya's largest and most progressive ethnic groups.

Spread across a large area of land which stretches on either side of the Athi-Sabaki River, much of their region is prone to drought – particularly the areas around Kitui in the eastern half of the territory.

Skilled hunters, marvellous woodcarvers and, in modern times, exemplary soldiers and police officers, the Kamba speak a language similar to the Kikuyu.

Historically, it appears that they settled in their present homelands in the last 500 years, swiftly establishing a thriving trade with their other neighbours – some of whom, like them, were newly-arrived. Thus were the communities established at the heartland of present-day Kenya.

Kamba wood carvings form one of the country's major craft industries: a visit to one of their carving cooperatives in Nairobi or Mombasa is salutary. Some 300 to 400 carvers squat on the floor deftly carving raw wood into exquisite shapes, individual artists working on a mass-production scale with some carvers jointly shaping elephants – one preparing the trunk, another the body, a third the legs.

Deeply superstitious, for many centuries they were renowned for the powers of their witch doctors. Today Kamba herbalists are widely respected for their skills with traditional medicines. In some instances, patients travel hundreds of miles in search of a cure for a debilitating disease or infertility.

Their chief seer, Masaku, predicted more than a century ago the arrival of the European and the advent of the railway – 'the long snake' – and the partition of the country. Corrupted, his name became that of the town, Machakos.

Traditionally, Kamba males could easily be identified by the sharpened points of the incisor teeth which were filed down in the upper jaw at the time of circumcision. Unlike the Kikuyu or Maasai, these proud and independent people approach adult life at two stages. Both boys and girls undergo a ritual initiation when very young, around the age of four to five, experiencing actual circumcision at puberty.

Gifted artists, fearless hunters, the Kamba play a significant role in Kenya's nation-building exercises. Two Chiefs of the Armed Forces staff were Kamba and many of the officers and serving men come from this enterprising society.

Above: Kamba children at play in a rock pool.

Opposite: Pumpkin—like gourds make versatile water containers when dried.

Right: Kamba women potters in the market place with their baked urns.

41

Two · People of the Lake and Highlands

Past, present, and future often meld together in an uncanny way in Kenya. What might appear fantasy is actually reality. A traditional dancer demonstrating the Luo warrior dance that, a century ago, was the prelude to deadly war, may, within the hour, be addressing a court in a three-piece pin-stripe suit. The sportsman hacking away obsessively at a series of golf balls to perfect his backswing might well be a Maasai who, leaving the golf club, returns to his traditional home to don the loose robes his ancestors favoured for thousands of years.

Nowhere does the past linger more vividly with the present than in western Kenya – from the high spine of the Mau summit down to the shores of the world's second largest freshwater lake, Victoria. Here the colourful threads of yesteryear are woven among the strands of the present to produce a stunning tapestry of contemporary life, which at one and the same time, is both ancient and modern.

In the far south-west, in the high hills beyond the Mara plains, alongside the Kenya-Tanzania border, bare-breasted young girls, in brief, traditionally embroidered skirts, follow the rhythmic beat of a drum. Women used to wear very tight armbands as decoration, but these are now banned as they can stop the flow of the blood. Dancing with them is a colourful young buck dressed in a dazzling array of feathers, skins, and fabrics, his feet weighed down with two enormous – eighteen centimetres (seven inches) thick – wooden clogs. He might be a teacher or a clerk; the girls are probably secretaries. But, at this moment, all are practising one of the many dances for which their people are famous. From time immemorial, the **Kuria** community have celebrated life with song and dance. They live in a wedge of hills bounded by the Maasai Mara in the east and

Kilkoris in the west. Even now, few roads lead into this remote and fertile location.

Made up of seventeen clans, the Kuria trace their origins back to both the neighbouring Gusii and Abagumba people. Physically, they were outstanding for their teeth which were filed down to fine points. In the male the two most prominent teeth were removed and some still carry this hallmark.

The majority of the Kuria – there are more than 100,000 in Kenya – live in Tanzania. But the Kenya community has been quick to respond to the progressive lead of its government. Half a century ago, these were the most notorious cattle rustlers in East Africa, far more rapacious even than their neighbours, the Maasai.

This way of life shaped the architecture of their homes. Fashioned on the lines of a fortress, they were made up of the huts of many units of the same family, each hut linked by a stout connecting fence made of poles and thorn branches, the centre of the palisade forming an easy-to-defend cattle compound. From behind this virtually impregnable wall, the Kuria would beat off the reprisal raids of the outraged Maasai and Kipsigis who came to recover their lost herds.

It could never be said that the Kuria marry in haste. Marriage is an extended affair – prolonged as much by the bargaining over bride price as by the drawn out preliminaries and the extended wedding ceremony itself. Before a couple are considered fully married, each must spend one night in the house of the other. After this, the bride is taken to a sacred stone shrine to undergo a ritual cleansing – ridding herself of all the evil she has caused in her short, young life.

In the evening of the same day, the groom goes to make the

Opposite: Kuria woman embroidering.

Right: Kuria male dancer leads young girls in traditional dance routine.

Right: Traditional and colourful Kuria earrings.

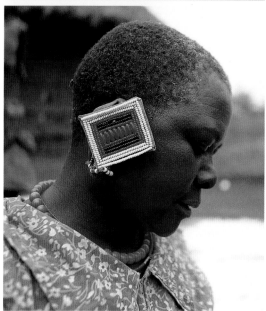

final instalment on the dowry – the first payment often begins while the bride-to-be is still at her mother's breast – and his sister escorts his wife back to his loving arms.

Both the Kuria marriage and circumcision ceremonies are enlivened by the dances for which the group is justly famous and which – unlike their cattle-thieving ways – they have not abandoned. In fact, from being ruthless and infamous rustlers, the Kuria have turned into exemplary citizens. Diligent farmers – their fields burgeon with crops and sleek cattle – they have transformed their market-places into townships. Now they have become centres of light industry and craft workshops.

Close kin of the Kuria, the 75,000 fisherfolk who make up the **Suba** community live on the islands and shores of Lake Victoria – from the Tanzanian border in the south to Homa Bay in the north. Renowned hippo hunters, the Suba used to stalk these ferocious animals at night as they grazed on shore. Moving stealthily, either alone or with a companion, they would creep close enough from downwind to plunge a harpoon into one of the three- to four-ton herbivores. Each harpoon was fastened to a long, strong rope with a wooden float. As the enraged, wounded animal returned to the water and sounded into the deeps, this float came adrift and rose to the surface.

In the morning, the marker was clue to the location of the creature, either dead or severely weakened by loss of blood. Hauled to the surface, it was finished off, if need be, with a flurry of harpoon thrusts. On rare occasions, in a show of bravado that sometimes proved fatal to the hunter and not the hunted, a young Suba buck would hunt down a hippo by day from his canoe. No matter the method though, each successful kill was an occasion to celebrate in song and dance.

Although they are now forbidden to hunt this protected species, the Suba remain excellent fishermen. Using long lines with many hooks, or drift nets which they lay from their traditional canoes, they haul prodigious catches from Victoria's waters. Few now use the traditional basket trap, a laborious method of fishing. More and more are turning to the sophisticated seine net, cast by hired labour from canoes and hauled in by hand from the shore.

Once this is done, Suba men disdain all interest in the fish. Their women take over – gutting the catch and either taking it to the market fresh, or drying it in the sun or over a fire.

These fishermen are also famous boat builders, and their craft are in great demand among other communities on the lake. Using fine mahogany, these sturdy, gaily-decorated craft – canoes and lateen-sailed fishing vessels – are a picturesque part of life on Lake Victoria.

The principal users are the fishermen among the 2.25-million-strong **Luo** who range along the shores of Victoria from Homa Bay in the south to Sio Port, close to the Uganda border, in the north. Inland, they extend well up the Nyando Escarpment and all along the fertile plains of Western and Nyanza Provinces. Many have migrated to fish, farm, or teach in every region of the country. The Luo, it is said, are like the water to which they have such a close affinity – flowing everywhere until they find their own level.

Formerly a cattle-herding culture, they adopted fishing when they migrated south from the Sudan centuries ago. As well as fishing, they also tend smallholdings – raising subsistence and cash crops, particularly sugar. Today much of their region, east of the lake, is the sugar belt of East Africa, kilometre after

kilometre of succulent cane, forming the basis of a massive agro industry.

Foremost among Kenyans for their fishing skills, the Luo exploit the waters of all Kenya's freshwater lakes, including the alkaline Turkana, and have also migrated to the coast to work the country's rich Indian Ocean fishing grounds.

In Victoria, mainly using gill nets and long lines, they draw in the prolific tilapia and other species, including the predatory and voracious Nile Perch whose introduction into the lake in the mid-1960s, it is claimed, has upset the lake's delicate ecosystem. The Luo also use a cunning basket maze trap which they lay down at the mouths of the many rivers and streams which flow off the hills of western Kenya into Victoria. The bewildered fish swim in easily enough, but can find no way out.

Offshore, out beyond Winam Gulf, their lateen-sailed boats, improvisations of the dhows introduced to these waters by the Arab slaves of the nineteenth century, are a familiar and fascinating sight. So are their sleek canoes, some now made of fibreglass and propelled by powerful outboard motors. This has done nothing to diminish Luo skills as watermen. Some of the most colourful sights on the lake are the annual regattas which villages hold. Watching the muscular oarsmen paddle their canoes through the waters, skins gleaming with spray, waves creaming back from the bows, is to study a picture of graceful but powerful symmetry in a scene as ageless as the lake itself.

Though the Luo do not practise circumcision – a test of valour as well as introduction to manhood – they have an ordeal equally severe for those at the threshold of manhood. Traditionally, at around adolescence the Luo draw five or six teeth from the lower jaw without any form of anaesthetic or painkiller. The initiate is under duress not to show any sign of flinching.

Polygamous, Luo husbands provide a personal hut for each wife. By tradition, new brides are abducted from their family by the husband's relatives – but only after he has paid enough of the dowry to get away with it. The abduction is the signal for a series of joyful ceremonies culminating in a wedding feast laid on by the husband.

When a Luo woman becomes pregnant she has to observe a strict number of taboos regarding customs and food. Twins, for instance, as in many Kenya societies until recently, were considered an ill omen. To make a new-born baby cry, it is doused in cold water or a relative might blow tobacco smoke up its nose.

Spirits, particularly those of ancestors, play an important role even today in Luo custom and belief. The group's top soccer team, many times Kenya league and cup winners, Gor Mahia, is named after one of the tribe's most sacred spirits. Witchcraft, mainly of the beneficial kind, is still practised in the more remote areas.

From their lofty hills, green and fertile and loaded with produce, the **Gusii** people, equally as fertile as their hills, look down on the Luo's southern lakeside resorts. So fecund they promise to break all known birth-rate statistics, at 700 people to the square kilometre the prolific Gusii have one of the highest population densities in Kenya, and the highest birth-rate in Africa. In fact, well above the national average of around four per cent, it is the highest in the world. From the 1979 census population of one million, their numbers increased dramatically in the nine years to 1988.

The country's sixth-largest tribe is split into many clans, each

Opposite: Luo fishing boats on the shores of Lake Victoria.

Below: Young Gusii child.

Opposite bottom: Brightly coloured finery of traditional Luo dancers.

of which forms a semi-independent local community. Heads of family used to judge minor social offences, invoking powerful curses as a final measure of disapproval. More serious crimes went before the elders, who sat as a council. Only they could perform the various rites and sacrifices which would bring divine retribution down on the head of the offender.

Less militant than their Maasai or Kipsigis neighbours, the Gusii suffered heavy losses of cattle in the early years of the century and developed a system of fortified enclosures similar to those of their other neighbours, the Kuria. Cattle were essential to Gusii society as a measure of wealth and a means of trading. Bride price was all paid for in cattle – around fifteen head a bride, an immense sum of wealth in those days yet, clearly, it has done nothing to daunt the Gusii's propensity for propagation.

While farming the verdant Kisii highlands, in recent years the Gusii have earned international renown at athletics and as artists and sculptors of the delicate white and rose-hued Kisii 'soapstone'. This skill with their hands is innate. For centuries the Gusii have practised a primitive but intricate form of trepanning. They treat patients – without anaesthetic – by tapping a small hole in the skull with all the precision of a modern surgeon performing a delicate brain operation. After relieving pressure on the brain, or performing even more delicate surgery inside the skull, the piece of skull is replaced. Many still alive swear to a miraculous recovery after such treatment.

Gusii trade extensively with their Luo neighbours, exchanging crops for such items as cattle, salt, and fish. They also craft iron hoes and spears for the Luo in exchange for basketwork and livestock.

Powerful and once warlike neighbours of the Gusii, the southernmost of Kenya's Kalenjin peoples, the 1.75-million-strong **Kipsigis** community have a love of cattle as passionate as that of the Maasai. Formerly moulded into a well-disciplined army made up of four major units, the Kipsigis have seven major age-sets, each covering around twenty-one years – creating a cycle beyond any mortal span, amounting to almost 150 years.

Each of the Kipsigis clans – and there are many – has its own individual totem, usually an animal, such as the elephant, or a bird, such as the crested crane. Fearless soldiers, the Kipsigis backed their Nandi brothers when that tribe took on the British just after the turn of the century, raiding and looting the railway which passed, uninvited and unwelcomed, through their land.

Like their age-sets, Kipsigis rituals are extended, drawn out affairs. Initiation, and other rites, can last from four to eight months. Circumcision, a critical point in life as it is in most Kenya societies, is carried out on both boys and girls.

Simply the starting point of a series of ceremonies into the customs and traditions of the tribe, youths are usually initiated around harvest time when there is enough grain to brew the beer the celebrants – family and elders – need to keep their spirits alive and joyous.

Prior to their initiation, young girls are cloaked from head to toe in a dress of blackened skins, embellished with clusters of bamboo beads, and led away to live in seclusion in an old woman's home. She has been chosen to instruct them in the virtues of the tribe and their duties as wives and mothers. After a series of secret rituals, the novitiates are circumcised and emerge as women – to be married almost at once.

When they drink beer at these festivities, the men sip from a

Above: Nandi women picking tea in the fertile Nandi Hills.

Opposite: Young Kipsigis girls in traditional leather skin circumcision dresses.

Right: Nandi elder with traditional earring.

common bowl, sucking it up through straws as much as two to four metres long made from a forest creeper, just as the Luo also do.

Living in settled areas, their days of nomadic pastoralism ended, the Kipsigis now earn the rewards and enjoy the virtues of arable farming as well as livestock herding. They are among Kenya's most productive farmers – rearing handsome, and high-yielding, dairy cattle and growing a wide range of subsistence and cash crops from potatoes, maize, cabbage, tomatoes, and onions to tea and pyrethrum. Like all Kalenjin people, Kipsigis make remarkable athletes. It was a Kipsigis who won Kenya's first Olympic Medal – Wilson Kiprigut Chuma, who took the bronze in the 800 metres at Tokyo in 1964.

Second only in numbers among the Kalenjin people to the Kipsigis, the **Nandi** early in the century earned themselves a reputation almost as fierce as that of the Zulu of South Africa, when they defied the British for a decade and more.

From around 1895 until 1905, Nandi *esprit de corps* and military tactics were so tenacious they seriously held up the British – both in establishing a road to Uganda where Imperial sights were set, and in the building of the Uganda railroad at the turn of the century.

Raiding down from their hillsides – rather like a bunch of dusky Sioux and Apache Indians on foot – the Nandi wrought havoc on the rail camps and rail works. They had a particular penchant for the copper telegraph wire which ran alongside the track and made excellent bracelets, armlets, and necklaces. Even after an armistice was arranged following the killing of their Chief, Koitalel, the Nandi were unable to resist plundering the telegraph wires. For years after, communications in this part of

Kenya were erratic.

Now living in scattered homesteads, the Nandi, while cherishing cattle and reflecting on a more pastoral and nomadic past, have long been cultivators, growing millet, maize, potatoes, pumpkins, and bananas. The heights of the Nandi Hills make them ideal for such cash crops as tea – many large and picturesque plantations roll from one hilltop to another – pyrethrum, tobacco, and coffee.

Like nearly all the Kenya people, the Nandi believe in one God, the Creator. He is known to them as *Asis*, the Supreme Being. But the spirits of departed ancestors can bring misfortune – so they have to be pacified with libations of beer, milk, and portions of food. Nandi spit to ward off bad luck. They also spit and salivate for good luck and as a form of blessing, much like the Kikuyu and other Kenya people. Spittle, sprayed on the chest and palms, is potent blessing – the epitome of honest dealing and elegant courtesy.

Ill-organized, divided into numerous sections, the Nandi lacked any real central authority throughout their history until the emergence, halfway through the last century, of the legendary chief, Barsobotwo. It was he who asserted himself and welded the group into the single cohesive community, capable of harrying the much better-equipped British for so long.

But perhaps among their fellow Kenyans, the Nandi are best known – and revered – for their seemingly endless stock of folklore, riddles, and proverbs.

As profligate as the Gusii, with a birth rate almost their equal and by 1988 a population density of well over one thousand people to the square kilometre, the seventeen disparate groups

Below: Ripe bananas on their way to a Luyia market in western Kenya.

Opposite: Notable boatmen, the Bunyala and Samia communities of the Luyia group show their paces in a racing canoe.

which make up the **Luyia** were well on the way to doubling their 1979 census population of 2.1 million. Expected to top more than three million at the next census in 1989, the Luyia occupy the fertile lands around Kakamega, scene of a 1930s gold rush and location of a rare remnant Congo rain forest with flora and fauna unique in East Africa.

Their communal name, Abaluyia, derives from their word for courtyard. When the clans gathered around the fires in the old days, any newcomer would be quizzed with the traditional question: 'To which courtyard (*oluyia*) do you belong?' In effect, asking: 'Which is your clan?' And with the formation of the Baluyia Welfare Association in 1940, the community name thus came into being.

Like their close neighbours the Luo, the Luyia also fish. But they are basically agriculturalists, growing sorghum, millet, sweet potatoes and other crops and rearing livestock. Their once well-fortified lands – surrounded by euphorbia hedges – and homes were ringed by defensive ditches and fortress-like clay walls, measures intended to keep out the foraging brigands of the Nandi, Iteso and far-ranging Maasai.

Once avid hunters – they used baited traps and snares, nets and pits – the Luyia were fine marksmen with bow and arrows and spears. Sometimes they would hunt smaller game in large groups with packs of dogs – a Kenya version of the more formal Anglo-Saxon hunt. Trophies, such as colobus monkey skin, giraffe and zebra tails, ostrich feathers, and wart hog tusks, became tribal regalia and, indeed, are still used for adornment at traditional events and as fly whisks and head-dresses. Not all Luyia practise circumcision. Some groups emulate the Luo test of courage – the drawing of the lower teeth without anaesthetic.

Passionately fond of music, the Luyia have also taken up soccer with an enthusiasm perhaps only matched by the Brazilians. Their club, renamed AFC Leopards after a government ordinance banning tribal affiliations likely to arouse emotions or retard development, is one of Kenya's most successful, along with the Luo's Gor Mahia.

The Luyias have assimilated into all levels of Kenyan society helping create a homogenous community and their skills as farmers, politicians, and sportsmen have greatly enhanced national life.

For many decades, the Luyia lived in fear of a ferocious group of warriors who had migrated south centuries before from the Sudan. Coming upon the fertile highland plains which encircle Mount Elgon, the **Iteso** abandoned their nomadic pastoralism and settled down – at the same time laying waste large stretches of the country and almost bringing the Luyia, particularly the Bukusu clan, to its knees.

These raids arose from the acquisitive urge of the Iteso to enlarge their cattle stockholdings. Today, however, the 150,000 strong community is fully assimilated into the national ethos.

Forming small villages scattered across the Busia and Bungoma districts of Kenya, the open-plan Iteso huts are surrounded by a covered verandah where the old men play frequent rounds of the traditional game, *bau*, a particularly skilful test of wit and intelligence, often perplexing to the western mind.

The naming of children in Iteso society is a curious and fascinating business. The name is chosen by the paternal grandmother, who visits the child, which is kept in seclusion from birth, when it is one week old.

The grandmother carries a gourd or calabash of newly-brewed

63

Opposite: Day's work done, an Iteso group indulge in social drinking from a traditional Iteso pot – using long straws, ipiina, *made from hollow creepers.*

Below: An Iteso market place.

millet beer. Placing her finger in the potent brew, she then puts the finger in the child's mouth, reciting the names of relatives renowned for their grace, prowess, or kindness. If the baby sucks strongly on the finger in response to the mention of a particular name, that is the one chosen.

However, should the baby fail to respond to any name the family consults the local seer to resolve the stalemate. He does it by naming two chickens, each with one of the most-favoured names, and placing the birds on a roost – usually the thatched roof of the house. The first bird to flutter from the roost decides which name the child will be given.

Drinking beer from a communal gourd during such celebrations, the Iteso, like the Kipsigis, draw up the liquid through exceptionally long tubes made from hollow creepers.

Music and dance is very much part of Iteso life. The tribe's five-stringed harp is a remarkable and beautiful instrument, its base formed of resonant wood, oblong in shape and completely covered with hide. With a hole near the top of this sound box, five strings of twisted tendons run from the tuning keys to the stem which curves out and upward. The Iteso, also skilful drummers, are renowned as well for their potter's art. Their delicately-sculpted clay figurines, fired in a traditional kiln after drying in the sun, are fine pieces of art.

Close neighbours of the Iteso are the four groups – **Bok, Bongomek, Kony**, and **Sebei** (in Uganda) – which make up the **Sabaot** community living on the fertile shoulders of 4,321-metre-high Mount Elgon astride the Kenya-Uganda border in the country's north-west.

They made their home on the mountain well above the fertile Uasin Gishu Plateau where they used to live for one reason only

– the constant raids of the Pokot, Karamojong, and Nandi, who made off with large numbers of their women and cattle. Indeed, the Kony (or Elgon Maasai) once lived at above 3,200 metres on Mount Elgon, probably the highest settlement anywhere in Africa. They kept sheep and goats there until just before Independence.

Higher altitudes ruled out their traditional livestock industry and they adapted to cultivation – only returning to the flatlands, which once were their home, at the advent of Kenya's Independence in 1963. While men herd the cattle, women milk the cows – a common cultural link through all Kalenjin societies.

Each segment of Sabaot society is divided into self-administered units: a number of scattered villages will form one unit with a council of elders which adjudicates on social and criminal issues. Largely obsolete now, the unit also used to acknowledge a seer, a post banned when the British took over Kenya.

Despite traumatic changes in Sabaot customs and cultures over the last century and a half, cattle remain a positive aspect of their life. As a form of insurance, cattle are contracted out to other groups on loan. Those who borrow them draw the milk and blood, but when one dies they must replace it on demand. Bride price is calculated in cattle and the husband also gives each wife a few head to start her own herd.

Three units form the basic society – clans, age-sets, and territorial entities. In the past the Sabaot used to appease the spirits with offerings of beer and food. But this practice, like the rank of warrior, is now redundant, resulting in the shortening of the gap between the circumcision ceremonies, which are now held every other year.

Progressive, well-adapted to the challenges facing Kenya as it moves towards the twenty-first century, the Sabaot have retained their athletic prowess. Among the world class runners who claim kinship with these highland folk is that master of the 3,000 – metre steeplechase, Ben Jipcho.

Endurance is inbred among all the Kalenjin – a heritage of high-altitude, hilly countryside, and the long distances which needed to be covered swiftly on foot. The community will remain a reservoir of national athletic talent for many decades to come.

Three · People of the Desert

Between the great highland massifs of central Kenya and Ethiopia, formed by the upheavals of the Great Rift Valley millions of years ago, lies a lowland of scrub, thorn, rock, and sand where little grows and few live. Spread mostly over northern Kenya, these deserts account for almost half of the country's land area – and give rise to communities whose resourcefulness and vitality has enabled them to utilize these badlands to their own advantage.

Only now are these once warring, nomadic desert tribesmen and their herds being drawn into the pervasive influence of modern Kenya through the development of social and community projects. New roads and townships, microwave communication links, and other infrastructures have brought this area closer to the rest of the country. Now, inevitably, new influences are crowding in upon the proud people of the desert.

Yet this last solitude remains a great experience. For three million years – from the time mankind first began to evolve in this region – little of the outside world intruded. Many still live a way of life as near to untouched existence as any in the world. These often fierce people use much the same techniques of survival, and have adopted much the same social structures, as their nomadic ancestors from Biblical days. 'For peoples who are pastoral,' says Colin Willock in *Africa's Rift Valley*, 'with social organizations based on communal grazing land and water supplies, the problems of living in a region where rainfall is erratic and grazing land sparse are almost insuperable.'

Almost but not quite, for few people anywhere in the world in any era have come to terms with such a melancholic, hostile environment to the degree of success achieved by these communities. There is a touch of resolution, a determined conservatism, an active indifference to other ways, and a total affinity with

their land, which marks all these semi-desert tribes.

Chief among these communities in stature, if not in numbers, are the **Tuken** people who live on a narrow wedge of the Rift Valley floor, bounded in the west by the Kerio River and along the rim of the lofty Tugen and Kamasia Hills to the east. They are often known as Tugen, too. The administrative centre of this community is the attractive town of Kabarnet. Living at two levels, the highland clans are more settled, less nomadic than their lowland kin who range around the Rift floor in the region of Lake Baringo. In fact, these highland folk have become assiduous agriculturalists as well as pastoralists.

A friendly and conciliatory society, the Tuken were among the earliest of Kenyans to take up employment – especially on farms around their southern boundaries. They also share their stock among themselves as a form of insurance.

Famed for their rainmaking ability, Tuken seers and medicine men were much in demand by the Nandi. They were also skilled in making a deadly poison from the stewed roots of a tree indigenous to their area. But, far from using it for murder, they traded it with their neighbours as a commodity.

Made up of seven age-sets, Tuken society once had an eighth – but it was dropped after suffering a humiliating defeat at the hands of their neighbours, the Keiyo, almost 200 years ago.

These age-sets move in cycles governed by the seven- to eight-year phenomenon of a rare desert bush coming into bloom: each alternate blossom, around every fifteen years, augurs a circumcision ceremony.

Living in circular huts built of cedar posts and made of mud-plastered walls and a thatched roof, every Tuken home has a place sacred to the family's ancestors at the base of the central post.

74

Most famous of this industrious, intelligent, and compassionate community is Kenya's second President, Daniel Toroitich arap Moi, who was born in a remote village in Baringo District. Tending his family's herds barefoot as a small boy, he grew up to become one of Africa's most distinguished statesmen and peacemakers.

It was a cattle raid on the Tuken which gave rise to one of the most colourful and dramatic stories in Kenyan folklore. Ambushed on their way home, before fording the Kerio River, a group of **Keiyo** rustlers had no means of escape except by leaping a five-metre-wide gap across a fifteen-metre-deep chasm. Thirty survived – the rest died either in the plunge to the rocks below or at the end of a retributory Tuken spear.

Though Kalenjin kinfolk of the Tuken, there is a long history of animosity between the two communities. Once, long ago, the Keiyo grazed and worked the land at the top of the Elgeyo Escarpment, a western wall of the Great Rift Valley often plunging sheer – in some places more than 1,524 metres — to the Rift Valley floor.

But, driven from their fertile fields by raiding tribes, today they live virtually by their fingertips on the precipitous ledges of the Elgeyo Escarpment, high above the craggy gorge of the Kerio River, now being tamed, like the Turkwel, by an ambitious hydroelectric scheme. Their new homelands extended no more than eighty kilometres in one direction and were only twelve to sixteen kilometres wide. It is only since Independence that these hardy people have started returning to the upper levels of the plateau – or down to the more level, but less fertile, valley floor.

But the ingenious terraced fields, set into the mountainside, still prevail, yielding crops of wimbi, millet, and maize to augment the tribe's traditional blood-and-milk diet.

*Opposite: Marakwet woman at
sundown milking.*

*Below: Pokot women's traditional
dance group.*

Famous for their blacksmiths – who, like the Turkana, belong to their own separate clan and are held in awe by the rest of the community – the Keiyo produced a formidable arsenal of hand combat weapons: a long and lethal spear, arrows, and fighting knives. These they would use in defence of their homes – traditionally set on a narrow ledge well beneath the escarpment and virtually unassailable.

They also used them for hunting elephant, buffalo, rhinoceros, and other animals for meat. The Keiyo were extremely adept and courageous hunters. Flushing an elephant on foot and turning it, a small group of spearsmen would wait in ambush in trees on the elephant trail.

Both boys and girls are circumcised. The women go into total seclusion after their initiation and wear a leather hood for one month. For three months after this their faces are covered by leather masks before they re-enter normal life wearing the costume of adult women.

Living in similar and perhaps more dramatic circumstances, the Keiyo's neighbours, the **Marakwet**, are divided into thirteen clans each with its own totems. They cluster along the impressive wall of the Great Rift Valley where it climbs 2,743 to 3,353 metres high – culminating in the magnificent Cherangani Hills.

Long tenants of this precipitous landscape, the Marakwet have developed amazingly compact smallholdings in the side of the cliff face – irrigated by an ancient but remarkably sophisticated system of canals fed by the waters of three rivers. Ownership of these canals is obscure and the community maintains and repairs them. Where there is a chasm, well-engineered aqueducts carry the water over and on. Astonishingly, this complex irrigation system has been in continuous use for more than 400 years – providing the Marakwet with lush crops of fruit and staples like millet and maize.

At least one Marakwet clan in the Cheranganis have become noted beekeepers. But livestock, because of the peculiar geography of Marakwet territory, is almost entirely limited to sheep and goats.

Courtship of Marakwet women takes place after their circumcision and is both stylish and graceful. The suitor visits the home to discuss marriage with the girl's parents but only after he has been given the go ahead by the girl. She acknowledges this by handing him the stick she was given to mark her initiation into womanhood. In return, he must hand over his spear and other weapons. When this is done he can begin negotiations with her parents.

For all this the couple still have to be particularly lucky to be matched: the Marakwet have many taboos against marriage – her totem group or age-set, for instance, may prove a barrier. And a Marakwet man can never marry a woman who belongs to the same age-set as his daughter. It is regarded as ritual incest.

If, however, the initial talks are favourable, the girl returns the man's visit to her parents by going to his house, where she assumes a pose of arrogant indifference bordering on contempt. This deliberate posture is designed to increase the offers of gifts and promises of livestock which her marriage will bring to her parents. Once the man pays a second visit to her home, the couple, in effect, become engaged. But marriage is not ritually complete until the woman has given birth.

Although the mother remains within the seclusion of her hut for one whole month after delivery, this is a happy occasion. It is said to the other children that she has gone to the home of the monkeys to ask for a child and, indeed, Marakwet mothers frequently refer to their children as *chereereny*, which in their

vernacular means 'my monkey.' Christened at birth, the child's name will reflect the time and the circumstances in which it was born.

Traditionally, the Marakwet have a widespread reputation for the skills of their midwives and surgeons who, like the Gusii, are particularly skilful at brain operations, using their own form of trepan. They also believe in one creator, whose name is the same as that of the Nandi, *Asis*.

Formerly known as the Suk, the **Pokot**, belligerent neighbours of the Marakwet, reach right down to the Rift Valley floor and fan out as far as Turkana – giving rise to two distinct cultures, just like the Keiyo, within the embrace of one distinct community.

Though related to the Kalenjin, the Pokot, through intermarriage and more frequent social intercourse with other tribes, have distinct differences from all other Kalenjin groups.

The pastoral group of the Pokot herd their cattle and flocks across the waterless scrub north of Lake Baringo, right up to the range of dramatic hills which forms the boundary with Uganda. Aggressive, they are often in conflict with the larger, more powerful Turkana and the Karamojong of Uganda. But their brethren, the plains Pokot, identical in all but habit, are agriculturists who farm the plains and upper levels of Pokot country and live in harmony with their neighbours.

Administered from Kapenguria, a small town high up in the Cherangani Hills where, in 1953, Mzee Jomo Kenyatta was tried – and sent down by the colonial authorities – in a rigged show trial, the tougher section of the Pokot share the Turkana's love of fierce and horrible fighting weapons: hooked finger knives, wrist knives, hand knives with sheaths, spears, the mandatory bow (arrows tipped with a lethal poison), and leather shield, combine to form a formidable complement of armaments.

Obsessed with a passion for cattle ownership, the Pokot, like the Maasai and Turkana, are extremely sentimental about each individual animal. In the 1980s one Pokot was so distraught when his favourite beast broke its leg that he committed suicide.

Horns of a favourite ox are hammered into distinctive, and often grotesque, shapes. Some walk about with one horn pointing forward, the other backward. All cattle carry a brand to identify ownership.

The Pokot are also remarkably unfussy in their diet. They eat the meat of any animal – except those which feed on carrion – augmented with blood, milk, and honey.

There is no fixed moment for circumcision. As soon as there is a large enough group of uninitiated youngsters, the man with the knife is summoned. The ceremony is brief and undistinguished. But they follow Maasai custom in spending a month alone in the bush shooting down small birds with blunt arrows. Dress is no real concern to the Pokot, except that the status of an elder is marked by the fact that he wears a cape of goat's skin. The elaborate scale of a head-dress, or hair fashioned in a particular way, is more indicative of Pokot social status.

Manhood comes early and simply to the **Turkana**, one of the most courageous and fiercest groups of warriors in Africa who number about 250,000. They roam 90,000 square kilometres of north-west Kenya beyond Lake Turkana.

The Turkana youth, aged between sixteen and twenty, is initiated in front of his elders. He is not circumcised. He has to kill a bull and there is a degree of finesse about the ritual. It is, for instance, an ill omen if the spear passes right through the beast.

Initiation means the youth has become eligible to take human life. He can only assume the status of warrior when he kills his

Above: Turkana women spend hours creating elaborate coiffeurs and braiding hair.

Left: Turkana elder with traditional nose jewellery.

Opposite: Turkana woman collecting water from shallow well in a dry river bed.

first human enemy, an event which he will mark by notching a scar on his right shoulder or chest.

From the day of his initiation a Turkana man is armed. His sponsor gives him a spear, other weapons, a stool which also serves as a headrest, and a pair of sandals. These will carry him across the burning sand and rock of the Turkana region in search of enemies to raid, and land and livestock to plunder.

Divided into nineteen different territories populated by twenty-eight clans, Turkana land is as ill-defined and loose-knit as its society. There is general disregard for the clan. Its main function is simply to regulate marriages to ensure each member of one clan marries into another. For the rest, the Turkana are indifferent to their own society. Indeed, clansmen are only one degree removed from total strangers.

Another characteristic of the Turkana is that they have only the vaguest notion of their own history. Their twin objectives concern only land and how to win it, and livestock and how to acquire it. They have pursued these aims with single-minded purpose for 300 years, from the time they broke away from the Karamojong group to settle in their semi-desert home.

Their territory stretches from Kapedo in the south to Sudan in the north, bounded in the west by the Karapokot Escarpment of Uganda and in the east by Lake Turkana, Mount Nyiru, and the Lehrogi Plateau – but the Turkana are still expanding. There are now thousands of them in the Wamba-Isiolo area.

Tending five species of livestock – cattle, camels, sheep, goats, and donkeys – the constant need of the Turkana is grass and water. Neighbours are always temporary. As pastures diminish, men go their own way. This state of affairs allows each individual to decide his own destiny, moving his settlement according to climate, vegetation and, of course, his own
86

inclination. A few have become disconsolate and disinterested fisherfolk. But, for the majority, the Turkana way of life is built around war and cattle.

The Turkana's formidable arsenal of hand-to-hand weapons consists of spears, shields, fighting sticks and clubs, razor-sharp wrist and finger knives and long, thin needles on which to skewer the opposition. More recently, they have acquired modern rifles. 'Among men for whom violence is still functional and honourable,' wrote one admirer of the Turkana, 'our guns were professionally admired as fine weapons.'

Turkana dress is little enough – usually a loose cloth. But without weapons, a warrior would feel naked. By using them, he earns the right to scarify his body just like a cowboy would put a notch on the handle of his six-gun – one on the right arm or chest denotes a male victim, one on the left a female victim. A warrior who has killed also earns the right to wear white ostrich feathers in his hair.

Women denote their status – either single or married – by the style and size of their necklaces, made of rings and beads.

Though fearless in all aspects of living, the Turkana are highly superstitious. They are great believers in dreams and place great faith in the arts of their diviners, who cast sandals to foretell a course of action. The manner in which a thrown sandal lies after it falls paints a decisive picture for the diviner.

Unfortunately for the peace and stability which should exist in the remote northern and north-eastern areas of Kenya, the hybrid **Dassanich** share the passion of their Turkana neighbours for war.

If they were anything less than perhaps Kenya's most ruthless community, Dassanich warriors might be regarded as transvestites. When a man is initiated – often in the late twenties or early

Above: Dassanich women and children at a waterhole in their searing desert homeland.

Left: Dassanich have now taken to fishing in the rich waters of Lake Turkana.

Right: Gabbra womenfolk loading water on their camels.

thirties – he pretends to be a woman. He spends his convalescence wearing a woman's skirt and ornaments and is treated just as the tribe treats a nursing mother. This shadowy transvestism runs through the entire sequence of male life – indicating, paradoxically, a powerful respect for the woman's role in a traditional male society.

If the Turkana notch their bodies to mark the number of human victims they have claimed, the Dassanich have an even more terrifying badge of valour. Traditionally, before a Dassanich can negotiate marriage, he must kill and castrate an enemy, placing the shorn genitalia around his neck like a necklace. No woman would consider marrying a man who does not carry this emblem of honour.

Yet each phase of Dassanich manhood is symbolic of the woman's life cycle. For the Dassanich the three major events in a woman's life are circumcision, the *dimi* ceremony which signals her emergence as a mother-to-be, and the birth of her first child. The men imitate this cycle. It helps underscore the pertinence of women – owning nothing, deciding nothing, yet every aspect of their lives foreshadows the rituals of manhood.

Divided into eight sections, the group is a relatively recent settlement of many disparate origins living a semi-nomadic existence along the lower reaches of the Omo River and, in Kenya, on the eastern shores of Lake Turkana south to Ileret and beyond. These people indulge in shifting cultivation with bored indifference, using the rich silt left behind by the seasonal October-November floodwaters of the Omo, Ethiopia's second-largest river. True pastoralists, they show more enthusiasm for fishing than agriculture.

Increasingly, during the late 1980s, the Dassanich were becoming assimilated into Kenya society reaching forward towards the coming century. Perhaps the last of Africa's Stone Age tribes, they now handle Space Age technology in the form of modern weapons and may soon make a significant contribution to the national ethos in more positive ways.

In doing so, they could also learn to benefit from the caring and positive social concern which their neighbours, the **Gabbra** nomads, display for each other in one of the most sophisticated societies to have evolved out of Kenya's dusty deserts.

Historically, little is known about this community which roams almost 50,000 square kilometres of Kenya – between the western slopes of Ethiopia's Mega Escarpment as far as Abore on the north shore of Teleki's Lake Stefanie (now Lake Chew Bahir), and south through the Chalbi Desert and the Dida Galgala Plains ('the Plains of Darkness') to Marsabit.

This environment has produced a unique social structure forming a well-orchestrated, well-co-ordinated, highly articulate pastoral community. Only one so resilient, and so well organized, could have overcome the threat of extinction which Gabbra society faced at the end of the nineteenth century when it suffered enormous losses from disease and raiding tribes.

Even towards the end of the 1980s, its hold on life is none too secure – the community numbers no more than 40,000 souls. Recent events like the 1977–78 Ogaden War in Ethiopia have also taken their toll of these fine-looking people who, with their high foreheads, skin oiled and glistening, appear as patriarchs from an Old Testament lithograph.

Permanent watering places are few and far between, and Gabbra society has developed as a response to both natural and man-made threats – either from failure of the rare rains or from hostile communities eager to seize stock and women. Using sophisticated techniques to exploit their scant water resources,

Above: El Molo youngsters fishing with harpoon on Lake Turkana from doum palm raft.

Left: El Molo youngster with water vessel.

Opposite: El Molo youngsters taking home their breakfast – a young crocodile.

the tribe's limited manpower nevertheless is always strained to the maximum.

As a consequence, the Gabbra have developed a unity which is completely the opposite of Turkana independence and individuality. Families stay together to form cohesive functional labour units. Indeed, an essential component of bride price is the duty of the groom to live with his bride's family for a year, and so close-knit are these families that often the groom's father goes with him to fulfil this obligation.

Entire families – parents, sisters, married sisters, sons and married brothers – will live as one unit, sharing domestic duties and locking up their separate herds each night in the same *boma* (compound). Marriage forms a lasting bond between families and clans, and these ties outweigh parochial loyalties.

Socially, Gabbra structures are highly sophisticated – developing a range of responsibility from an early age until reaching full maturity, before a serene retirement as a community sage without any obligations.

Generation sets are based on a seven-year cycle prone to interruption by natural disaster or war, and provide an organized hierarchical structure for law and order.

Less a tribe, more an unfortunate group, the **el Molo**, who live in the south-east corner of Lake Turkana, were once wrongly described as the smallest tribe in the world. Now numbering more than 500, this small collection of dropouts from other groups has virtually abandoned its Stone Age ways and moved towards the mainstream of Kenya society.

El Molo legend has it that all the creatures of Lake Turkana are herds which belong to them, but were scattered by an act of misfortune. Now, forbidden to hunt the hippo and the crocodile – an act of singular bravery by either individuals or small groups

94

– they have even quit the small islands which are their traditional homes and burial grounds.

Shrouded in folklore, mystery, and legend, their only worldly possessions are their sticks and string homes, their fishing rafts and implements. Yet, for centuries, overcoming much greater misfortune than prouder, but certainly never more resilient communities, the el Molo have survived. Suffering from an ill-balanced diet caused by too much fluoride in the water, bandy-legged and tooth-stained, in the last century their Neolithic lifestyle has fascinated all who have encountered it.

Unlike their neighbours, the el Molo are basically monogamous, but due to intermarriage with women from other tribes, especially the Samburu, their numbers underwent a dramatic revival in the seventies and eighties. The el Molo community as an entity was on the edge of extinction in the two decades before this transformation.

Another aspect of their survival can be attributed to their adaptability. In the space of fifty years, for instance, their language changed so completely that only the oldest living men remembered the words of their original language – the middle-aged knew only that there had been another language, while the young were unaware of the fact.

The majority of the el Molo now speak Samburu, the language of the tribe to which the group is most closely affiliated, although shared cultural traits exist with the Rendille, including the same deity and the same burial practices.

All el Molo fish adroitly from shore or from crude doum palm log rafts which quickly become waterlogged. Yet few el Molo are lost in the sudden squalls which whip down on the south-eastern end of the lake off Loiyangalani, from the lofty heights of Mount Kulal, turning the Jade Sea into a turbulent, storm-tossed

Below: Black robed initiates of the Samburu returning from Lake Kisima after collecting water as a blessing for their circumcision.

Right: Samburu bride.

Opposite bottom: Young Samburu warrior on a month's seclusion in the bush after circumcision.

inland ocean with vicious waves.

Using spears, harpoons, nets, and basket traps, the el Molo catch prodigious numbers of fish. Their lines are made by the women from doum palm fibre, and the tribal smiths forge the hooks and harpoon heads. The women also practice a crude form of pottery.

The 100,000–strong **Samburu** – the word means 'butterfly' in the Maa language – who occupy the lush highland pastures and moist forests of the 1,800–metre-high Leroghi Plateau, are close kin of the larger Maasai group, but broke away centuries ago to settle in this area. They are known as butterflies by other groups because of their constant movement.

The southernmost boundary of Samburu territory lies just beyond Rumuruti. Bounded by Mount Kulal in the north, stretching through Laisamis to the Ewaso Ngiro river and west along this baseline as far as Maralal and the Leroghi Plateau, the Samburu lay claim to some 28,000 square kilometres of rugged mountain and desert. In some areas, they share a common and remarkably harmonious tenancy with the Rendille people.

The Samburu herds flourish on the often lush pastures promoted by the rains which fall on their highland regions. All the tribe's social structures are built upon cattle and their ownership. Pastoralists pure and simple, the Samburu cultivate nothing in the way of cash or food crops. They keep small herds of camels in their northern territory and large numbers of sheep and goats.

The Samburu's age-set system, as intricate as that of the Maasai, is designed solely to perpetuate the elitism of the elders. It is therefore elaborated in such a way as to control the wayward warriors – in a series of ceremonies which continue throughout life.

It is as well to understand this philosophy. The virtues of their nomadic life are those of the Old Testament. An eye for an eye and a tooth for a tooth is pertinent justice in the land of the Samburu. The same outlook applies to moral judgements. Senior citizens are not regarded as senile. Therefore, as in Maasai society, and most Kenya societies, elders have a particularly valued place in Samburu society. The point is worth making, for the Samburu lack any kind of formal political or ritual rule.

Although culturally related to the Samburu in many ways, the **Rendille** nomads who roam the Kaisut desert below the Leroghi Plateau as far as Kulal and Marsabit have only a limited kinship – mainly through marriage.

Truly pastoral, the community shares a common boundary with the Samburu in the region of the ol Doinyo Lenkiyo, Ndoto, and Nyiru Mountains, ranging from there through the Kaisut Desert to the south-east shores of Turkana and across to Marsabit – somewhere between 15,000 to 37,000 square kilometres of arid, infertile land – most of it less than 600 metres above sea level.

This harsh terrain, where rainfall rarely exceeds eighteen centimetres a year, makes herding the Rendille camels always an arduous, and sometimes dangerous, task. Children are apprenticed to it from the time they can walk until the age of about thirteen. After that, they keep herd on their own.

These early years serve as an education in the unique values of Rendille society. To these highly superstitious people, one of the most significant taboos is that of a second son born on a moonless Wednesday of the Rendille week. Even today such an infant is laid out in the bush minutes after birth, fodder for the hyaena. Rendille believe such a son is a curse and will bewitch

Above: Rendille bleeding camels as the Maasai do cattle.

Left: Mixed with milk and left to ferment, camel's blood makes an intoxicating brew.

Opposite: Rendille couple lead their camel home through the stony Kaisut desert.

the first-born brother and cause his death, or steal his inheritance.

One year after circumcision, which takes place after intervals as long as fourteen years, all the initiates meet for a week-long gathering on the shores of Lake Turkana when they are given their age-set name. They live in a camp so large it has a radius of five kilometres. Rendille society as a whole celebrates two annual festivals – the occasions set, like the Gabbra festivals, by the movement of the moon. This is the time to happily slaughter a camel, the elders daubing their bodies with its blood.

For a Rendille girl to become pregnant before she is circumcised is to bring grave dishonour on her family and herself. In days of yore, the girl and her lover were simply tied together on a camel which was then driven off the top of a sheer cliff face. Today she is simply thrown out of the house to fend for herself.

Yet Rendille indifference to social and economic progress remains monumental. Their traditions, including their unique initiation ceremonies, endure because they refuse to allow their erosion.

Four · People of Sand and Sea

East of a straight line from Kenya's southernmost border post, Lunga-Lunga, to Moyale on the Ethiopian border in the north, lies a broad swathe of lowland Africa, mostly desert, with some savannah and open grassland, none of it more than 500 metres above sea level. Much easier to travel across than Kenya's high hinterland, in the old days it was here and at the coast that most visitors made their first contact with Kenyan communities.

The lowland tribes of Kenya have been exposed to external influences for centuries. The first waves of Islamic migrants arrived here more than a thousand years ago, bringing with them the cultures of Arabia and the Orient. Today, the majority of these lowland peoples, mainly hardy nomads, are Muslim, though some practise their own age-old religion, usually monotheist in concept and form. These societies have many time-proven virtues – hardiness, independence, and thriftiness foremost among them.

None value these virtues more than the 90,000 people who make up the **Boran** community which ranges far and wide through north-eastern Kenya. Descendants of the Oromo-speaking peoples of Ethiopia, the Boran moved south into what is now Kenya around the turn of the century, settling down to a semi-nomadic life in towns like Moyale and Marsabit – and even Isiolo, nestling at the northern foot of Mount Kenya. They were driven this far by the rapacious demands of the expansionist Ethiopian Emperor, Menelik II.

Divided into five generation sets with four initiation cycles of eight years each, the wheel of Boran society turns full circle every forty years. Though the southernmost Boran have been converted to Islam through close contact with the Somali, the

Left: Boran elder.

Left: Boran craft water vessels out of stitched camel hide.

Opposite: Boran woman with a skin and cowrie shell dress.

majority still practise their ancient faith, in which they communicate with the supreme deity, *Wak*, through prayers and sacrifices under the direction of a priest. This ritual leader lives in a much larger house than the others – a flat-topped structure made of grass and foliage, laid over a framework of withies.

In Boran society, snakes are considered powerful spirits and reptiles are kept in bamboo containers. The strange significance attached to snakes is also paradoxical. While one section kills all snakes except the puff adder, another section kills no snakes but the puff adder!

Even now, the mystery remains. Almost all Boran life is a ritual of unexplained symbolism nowhere more complex than the affair of celebrating birth. The naming of a new child develops into a whole series of time-consuming rituals.

The Boran establish the status of warrior in exactly the same way as the Turkana: a man may use this title only when he has made his first kill, either human or that of a lion or elephant.

But when a warrior becomes an elder, he abandons violence completely – never again to carry weapons, provoke people or quarrel unless, of course, pushed beyond the limit by insult and provocation.

Boran women may be circumcised at any time without ceremony, by infibulation. The bride is paid for in cattle, tobacco, or dried coffee.

Their neighbours around Moyale form another group which also fled Ethiopia at around the same time to avoid the harsh tribute extracted by Menelik II. The first **Burji** emigrant to the country was probably a man called Hille Ume, who crossed into Moyale in 1906 – the first of several thousand who came to ply their trade as shopkeepers in this border town, and in Marsabit farther south.

Once agriculturalists, unlike the cattle-keeping Boran, the Burji grew teff, a wheat-like grain indigenous to Ethiopia, beans, and other vegetables in their former hillside homes around Gara Burji. Gracious and sophisticated, the Burji have also long woven cloth from the cotton which they spin themselves, disdaining animal skins. Using crude hand looms, the Burji fashion handsome textiles, turning them into elegant robes and dresses. Now a dying craft, it was once common to see the old men and women seated under the eaves of their distinctive huts in Moyale, working at their spindles and looms.

A law-abiding and constructive society, over the first eight decades of this century the Burji became an important source of farm labour in the Moyale and Marsabit district and prime workers for road building and house construction. Now some of these thrifty people have moved as far as Nairobi, where they have become successful traders.

Practising circumcision between the ages of ten to fifteen, the tribe has eight age grades under the leadership of a hereditary spiritual and political chief who passes on his power to his son. During an impressive ritual at the time of his death, his ring is transferred to his heir and the old man buried with his ivory jewellery. At once, his heir is expected to choose a high-born bride to become the tribal queen.

A Burji girl's upbringing determines her suitability as a wife. No single girl can leave the home without a chaperon and she is constantly watched by her mother and other close female relatives, usually her aunts.

Should a girl remain single for too long, however, she becomes a severe embarassment to the family. When shopping for a bride, the potential groom takes into account the girl's social status, caste and reputation.

Similar constraints about a potential bride prevail in **Somali** society. Around 400,000 of these handsome, pastoral nomads claim Kenyan citizenship and ancestry in the sandy flatlands that join Somalia and north-eastern Kenya.

Their migration into what is now Kenya goes back centuries. Driving out the smaller communities which stood in the way of their access to water and pasturage, the militant Somali spread right across Kenya's eastern lowlands. Divided into two sections – aristocrats and commoners – they are utterly dependent on the precarious and unpredictable grazing and rains of the areas in which they live.

Each extended family moves across the desert as a single mobile unit, their affairs controlled by a council made up of all the heads of family within the unit. Quarrels over camels, women, water, and grazing are frequent. Moral and physical injuries are settled by the council with an elected chief as the final arbitrator.

Adopting Islam centuries ago, the Somali practise the limited polygamy – up to four wives – allowed them. The first and senior wife exerts a real and judicious authority over her co-wives, tempering it with indulgence to the youngest and most favoured bride. Each wife controls some part of the husband's herds of camels, cattle, and sheep, although he remains the legal owner.

Both sexes undergo initiation. There is less ceremonial attached to this than in the highland tribes. Circumcision of
110

men, which has a religious aspect, is now being carried out earlier than before. Boys as young as eight undergo the cut. Young girls are always infibulated early – around six to eight year, the vulva stitched together with thorns after the clitoris has been removed.

The groom's choice of a wife has to be approved by his kinsmen before bride wealth can be paid. In Somali society this is reciprocal – the groom receiving gifts from the bride's family, though on a much smaller scale than those he gives.

Highly articulate and politically conscious, Somali unity is built around family loyalty and formal contracts. Those that control water and grazing maintain their status through force if necessary. The indemnity for taking one man's life was two camels; that for a woman, one camel.

Among the same group of Oromo-speaking peoples as the Boran and Burji, the **Orma** migrated south from north-east Kenya long ago, well before the most recent waves of migrants, only to come under subsequent pressure from the Somali.

As a consequence, the Orma moved even farther south to herd their cattle on either side of the Tana River – between Garissa to the west and Garsen to the east.

Numbering less than 50,000, these tall, handsome, and slender people are pastoralists who, when drought is severe, often clash with the Kamba over the use of water-holes. The northern area of Tsavo East National Park, formerly their dry weather range, is now forbidden to them. The Orma's distinctive herds of white, long-horned Zebu cattle are among the finest indigenous cattle in Africa. Some Orma own more than a thousand head. Such wealth elevates a man to an elite status

Below: Somali herdsmen waters his herds of goats, cattle, and camels at a desert waterhole.

Below: Somali child on one of the family camels.

within the tribe.

Like the Dassanich, Orma warriors are circumcised late in life. Marriages are conducted with a great deal of ceremony and elan. Drums beat as the bride is formally escorted to the groom's house, where he sacrifices an ox or sheep and, catching the blood in his hand, pours it over his future wife's breast and right foot, then on his own forehead before smearing the remainder on the centrepost of the house.

This is a potent omen, an irrevocable symbol of the oath of marriage. It cannot be performed unless he has paid the bride price. In the evening relatives and friends celebrate the beauty of the bride in song and keep vigil throughout the night. Proof of the bride's virginity is greeted with prolonged celebration. Though polygamous, many Orma men prefer to remain monogamous – sacrificing the prestige that goes with several wives and children. Rich Orma, however, often keep acknowledged concubines.

Orma funerals are also conducted with style and dignity. The family will inflict wounds on themselves, scratching their cheeks and body as an indication of their grief. As the body is wrapped in its shroud and carried off on a bamboo litter to the grave, the women resist its removal – lamenting that no more will the man make love to them, and praising the virility he showed when alive.

Downstream from the Orma pasturelands lies the home of the 50,000 or so people who make up the **Pokomo**, agriculturists who work the land immediately alongside the Tana where it is enriched by the flood silt and easily irrigated.

Perhaps unique among Kenya farmers, the Pokomo, though

not assiduous workers like their upcountry cousins, usually harvest three crops a year. These range from coconuts to pineapples, tomatoes, other fruits and most vegetables, providing a rich, varied and healthy diet. In the 1980s, the Pokomo also began earning profitable sums from their new tobacco plantations.

Villages of ten to fifty domed circular huts, made of poles, liana ropes, and grass thatch and raised on stilts, border the waterfront of a typical Pokomo village, surrounded by a palisade of heavy wooden poles three metres high.

Expert swimmers and boatmen, the Pokomo navigate their dugout canoes on the Tana's swirling waters with considerable skill and dexterity. Skilled hunters, they are no longer allowed to take crocodile or hippo, which were once an important staple of their diet, but they still fish from the dugout using hook and line, and from the river banks using the wicker traps and weirs.

Divided into two groups, the upstream group practises circumcision, the downstream group does not. Bride price is paid in food, and the mother of the bride is festooned with gifts of copper bracelets and given butter and ointments.

The downstream community, closer to the coast, came under the influence of the early Christian missionaries, but their way of life changed little until the 1980s. Only then, with extensive settlements, development schemes, and improved communications, did these picturesque people, whose fleets of canoes serve as waterborne taxis on the wide sweep of the Tana, finally enter the mainstream of Kenya society.

Yet, for some Kenyan communities, any change brings an inevitable collapse in traditional structures. None is more

Left: Pensive Orma woman in traditional dress and jewellery.

Below: Pokomo boatmen in their dugout canoes on the Tana River.

vulnerable than the Okiek and their kindred group, which have been hunting and gathering in the coast hinterland from time immemorial, the **Boni**.

Two similar groups are the **Wata**, sometimes known as the **Waliangulu**, and the **Dahalo**, descendants of primal hunting communities which evolved in this region literally thousands of years ago – the first real Kenyans whose ways of life changed little until the final decades of this century. The Dahalo share affinities of language and culture with the 'click-speaking' Bushmen of southern Africa, the Khosian community. And they may have ethnic links with similar little-known groups in northern Tanzania, the **Iraqw** and the **Tatoga**.

Until the 1960s, the Boni group was made up of a dozen or more nomadic units. Then, Somali brigands raiding in their region upset the balance of their life and for safety they settled permanently along the coast hinterland.

Traditionally, the Wata (or Waliangulu) still roam most of the vast hinterland from Kipini near the Somalia border to Voi and beyond.

With a traditional economy based on hunting and gathering roots, wild fruits, and honey, the combined population of the Boni group numbers only around 5,000. But now that they have taken to agriculture their unique culture is in danger.

The Boni are probably the greatest surviving exponents of bushcraft in Kenya. Watching the women follow the rains, digging for roots, berries and fruits is to see a pattern of life which demonstrates the resilience and resourcefulness which has enabled this group to survive natural disaster after natural disaster through the millenniums.

Even with these scant resources, they show it is possible not only to survive but to enjoy good health. They pay remarkable regard to anything, even the stems of wild plants. Chopped up, the pith of these is a valuable source of nourishment during famine and drought. It is fermented, washed in hot water, and ground into flour to make a sustaining porridge.

The Wata are perhaps Kenya's, and Africa's, most renowned trackers and hunters. Long before English archers defended the Plantaganet crown of England against the French at Agincourt, the Wata had been using the long bow for hundreds of years to bring down elephant.

Thousands of years of culture also envelop the Wata's north coast neighbours – the cultured and sophisticated people of the **Bajun, Swahili**, and **Shirazi** communities, which number altogether around 60,000 to 70,000. Their past came to a glorious apogee long ago in a fusion of cultures with Arabia and the Orient and, more recently, Europe. It was around the eight century when the first Islamic traders called at the coast of East Africa, first in the north around the Lamu archipelago where the 45,000 people of the Bajun people still live a way of life little changed in the last thousand years. Even today, no cars disturb the peace and quiet of Lamu Island.

Here the predominant influence is that of Islam – the women cloaked in the discreet all-embracing black veil, known as the *bui-bui*, only their eyes gazing out on the wider world. Sharing a common religion, the Bajun, Swahili, and Shirazi also have a common culture and a common language. Swahili, a mixture of Bantu and Arabic words, is one of the great living languages of the twentieth century and the *lingua franca* of eastern Africa; a

Below: Exquisitely carved ivory siwa *played by a Bajun on the Lamu archipalego. It's now part of Lamu Museum's collection of traditional musical instruments.*

Right: Shy, sloe—eyed Swahili women in the traditional bui bui costume.

Right: Not so shy Swahili matriarch of Lamu.

result, like the people themselves, of centuries of immigration and trade, transmigration, and miscegenation. Up to twelve local dialects of the Swahili language are spoken along Kenya's north coast.

The Bajun claim kinship with the Arabian peoples from Hijaz, the Persian Gulf, and South Arabia, and the 7,000 or so Shirazi, a scattered maritime and agricultural people, trace their lineage back to the tenth-century occupants of Persia. Long ago, they say, they made up the aristocracies and rulers of the tiny Ozi sultanates of Shaka, Mwana, Ungwana, Malindi, and Mombasa, but few anthropologists support this folklore.

Fishing and farming are the main pursuits of this group of people, although wood carving and boat building – beautifully crafted dhows which are such a feature of Indian Ocean life from Kenya to the Gulf – are major industries in Lamu. Kenya's coastal people have indulged in shifting agriculture since time began. Bush fires for land clearing are recorded in a second-century history of the coast, written by the Greek sailors. Other craft industries include metal, leather, and basket work and rope-making from coir, a by-product of the coconut plantations.

Almost one million people – the **Giriama, Digo, Duruma, Chonyi, Jibana, Ribe, Kambe, Rabai**, and **Kauma**; the 'nine tribes' – make up the **Mijikenda** group which has lived at the coast for around the last 300 to 400 years, from just south of Lamu all the way down the coast to Vanga on the Tanzanian border.

Colourful and friendly, the Mijikenda are passionately fond of music and dancing. Sharing a common language, culture, and history, the Giriama is the largest of the nine 'tribes' – occupying most of the area around Kilifi, which lies between Malindi and Mombasa. The various groups only developed a close common identity as recently as 1940 – somewhat like the Luyia of western Kenya.

Highly superstitious, they practise many forms of clandestine witchcraft, and traditionally their villages are protected by burying a pot full of charms, potions, and amulets in the ground near the house where the village elders meet. Practising circumcision with a number of age-groups, the Mijikenda herald initiation with powerful displays of drumming on a special drum called the *mwanza m'kulu*.

Much of Mijikenda power is vested in powerful 'masonic' groups, in which membership is strictly controlled and fees are payable. Different forms of emblems, dress, and decoration signify membership of each particular secret society.

Once lethargic farmers – the Mijikenda grew a variety of crops and fruits and kept livestock – much of their economy was based on trade. Straddling the trade routes into the interior during the last three centuries, they were well able to exploit their situation.

In the years since Independence, however, the Mijikenda have diversified their interests and quickened their development. They have adapted to the tempo of the burgeoning tourist industry to develop successful commercial farms supplying coast hotels with much of their fare, also moving into livestock breeding with co-operative ranching.

Their beautiful loaf-shaped, intricate houses, rectangular in shape, with their distinctive *makuti* thatch roofing, are familiar sights to most tourists to the Kenya Coast, who also fall under the spell of the exciting Giriama dancing and music.

Left: Mijikenda group at water well on north Kenya coast – part of a community made up of nine 'tribes'.

Below: Traditional Giriama homestead on the Kenya coast.

Right: Digo drummers.

Right: Elderly Segeju woman of Kenya's south coast.

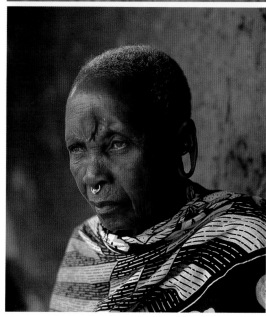

The wind instruments used by the Digo and Duruma are among the most sophisticated traditional music instruments in Africa. Indeed, the Digo have a superb flute called the *chivoti*. Mijikenda drumming adds an exciting and lively accompaniment to this ensemble of instruments and they have developed many forms of percussion instruments.

Four hundred years ago the Mijikenda's neighbours, the **Segeju**, one of the least known today of Kenya's tribes, were as formidable as the Maasai – frequently at war, herding large numbers of cattle, braiding their hair with ochre, wearing skins and living on a basic diet of blood and milk.

So ferocious were these people, they formed an alliance with Vasco da Gama's Portuguese settlers and helped drive away the marauding Zimba cannibals from Mombasa. They were mentioned glowingly in a history written by a Portuguese cleric, Father Monclarco, in 1569, in which he called them Mosseguejos.

Today they are far from warlike – now reverent followers of Islam, settled and numbering fewer than one thousand people in all, their quiet, reflective way of life is a far cry from their turbulent and tempestuous past.

Believed once to have lived around the foothills of Mount Kenya, the Segeju drifted east many centuries ago, reaching their apogee at the end of the sixteenth century when they conquered Malindi and Mombasa. Their reign was brief. Soon they were driven out to begin a final drift south, down the coast, into the limbo of Kenya's forgotten cultures and peoples. Now this remnant group lives close to the Tanzanian border at

Shimoni. The largest group of survivors actually lives on in Tanzania.

From pastoral nomadism and war, the Segeju have become skilled craftsmen especially renowned for their plaited mats and hangings.

Their homes are well-ventilated, roomy, and very solid. These coral-rag and lime plastered huts are roofed with *makuti* thatching – neat, smart, and typical of the south coast. The few surviving Segeju have assimilated well into the modern coastal cultures with little time for outdated traditions of the past. Many of their smallholdings have been abandoned.

The new generations have moved to Mombasa to work in industry, commerce and tourism – facing towards a future which all the *Beautiful People of Kenya,* while conscious of a rich and rewarding history, can share as one people, one nation on the only sure road to a stable and prosperous future.

Overleaf: Sundown over Lake Victoria.